Food for Thought . . .

Building a strong nutritional foundation for children is one of the most important tasks we face as parents and teachers. *The Fruit Bowl* and *Vegetable Soup* present wholesome eating habits in a highly inviting, interactive and visual format. After all, "we are what we eat" and the best time to learn and integrate this basic concept into our lives is when we are young so that we have the best start on total health for a lifetime.

Ann Louise Gittleman, M.S.
Certified Nutrition Specialist/Author
Your Body Knows Best and
Get The Sugar Out

There is no better way to have healthy people than to start at the very beginning. We have abundant evidence to prove that fruits and vegetables are the basic edibles that serve to maintain our immune system, slow down the severity and frequency of infections and prevent or delay the onset of cancer and heart disease. The healthy start is right here in *Vegetable Soup* and *The Fruit Bowl*. Sure, occasionally let the little tykes have snacks at birthdays and parties, but also have them grow fruits and vegetables in the backyard and help with their preparation. We must teach our children to eat fresh foods, not the sugary junk found in the middle of the grocery store.

Lendon H. Smith, M.D.
Author, How to Raise a Healthy Child

A child's health starts in the womb. Healthy choices through pregnancy must be followed by teaching our children to make their own healthy choices as well. *Vegetable Soup* and *The Fruit Bowl* help parents and teachers introduce children to the connection between what they eat, how they look, feel and perform. This early education will help prepare them to make those choices.

Earl Mindell, PhD
Author, Earl Mindell's Vitamin Bible and
Earl Mindell's Anti-Aging Bible

Take your children grocery shopping occasionally. Spend most of your time in the produce department and make each trip a learning experience. Show them the most intensely colored fruits and vegetables and explain that these are the best. Do this often. Children relish this information and will always remember what they learn here.

Charles Attwood, M.D., F.A.A.P.
Author, Dr. Attwood's Low-Fat Prescription for Kids
and the audio series, *The Gold Standard Diet*

Food for Thought...

Disease begins in childhood. All the studies that have been done on the artery health of children tell us, beyond a doubt, that the beginnings of heart disease are present in our children today. We must, as parents, teachers and health professionals, get our children on safer diets and into the habit of eating lots of fresh fruits and vegetables. *Vegetable Soup* and *The Fruit Bowl* help us lead them in the right direction.

William P. Castelli, M.D.
Medical Director Framingham Cardio-Vascular Institute,
Columbia Metrowest Medical Center,
Adjunct Associate Professor of Medicine
Boston University Medical School

The old saying "you are what you eat" today takes on new meaning as modern scientists begin to unravel the myriad ways in which the consumption of fruit, vegetables, whole grains, beans, nuts and seeds build and maintain the health of our magical bodies. Our current epidemic of poor bone health and the growing trend toward increased, needless bone fractures, for example, could be reversed for future generations if all children were to enjoy optimum nutrient intake and abundant outdoor exercise.

Susan E. Brown, PhD
Director, The Osteoporosis Education
Project, Syracuse, NY
Author, Better Bones, Better Body:
A Comprehensive Self-Help for Preventing,
Halting and Overcoming Osteoporosis

I think that *Vegetable Soup* and *The Fruit Bowl* is the finest children's book written on the benefits of produce related to health. With the abundant supplies and varieties of fruits and vegetables available today, it has never been easier to get our kids to "eat fresh and stay healthy."

Tony Tantillo, *The Fresh Grocer*
KPIX Channel 5 News,
San Francisco CBS Affiliate

The importance of books like *Vegetable Soup* and *The Fruit Bowl* has never been more evident. Children's tastes are adaptable and childhood habits tend to last a lifetime contributing to health or chronic disease as they age. We must get our children on the right track for long term health by getting them in the habit of eating lots of fresh fruits and vegetables.

T. Colin Campbell, PhD
Director, China-Oxford-Cornell Study on Diet and Health
Chaired Professor, Nutritional Biochemistry,
Cornell University

Reach out with warmth and wisdom to bring the message of health to your child. This book, *Vegetable Soup* and *The Fruit Bowl,* is a must!

Marilyn Diamond, *Author*
Fit For Life and *Fitonics*

THE FRUIT BOWL

A Contest Among the Fruit

Dianne Warren
and
Susan Smith Jones

Illustrated by:
Amy Sorvaag Lindman

All the fruit have gathered.
The Bowl is about to begin.
Which is your favorite fruit?
Who do you think will win?

The first contestants are APPLES,
Red, yellow and green.
As salads, snacks, and juices
They make a winning team!

The APRICOT has landed,
A golden springtime treat.
When dried she's tops in Vitamin A
And really hard to beat.

The AVOCADOS have arrived,
The Fuerte and the Haas.
As sandwiches and dips
It's hard to see a loss.

The yellow BANANAS are next,
They always come in a bunch,
In smoothies and in sandwiches
They make a delicious lunch.

Here comes the BERRY family,
Raspberry, Blue and Black,
As snacks, in jams and juices,
There's nothing that they lack.

Coming next is CANTALOUPE,
A summer breakfast delight.
So full of important vitamins,
A winner bite after bite!

The **CHERRIES** have entered The Bowl
And expect to win a prize.
They are so very sure
There's no better fruit for pies!

**The DATE came from the desert
Where he grows on tall palm trees.
He's so good in cookies and shakes,
He thinks he'll win with ease.**

The GRAPES know they will win,
For they have so many uses:
As snacks, in jams and salads
Or a variety of juices.

The LEMONS and LIMES are excited.
They think they're the "Fruit of the Hour".
I know for sure they'd win the prize
Awarded for being most sour!

MANGOES are one of the tastiest
Fruits from tropical places.
It's best to eat them with water nearby,
For the fruit ends up on our faces!

Hooray for the NECTARINE,
A close cousin of the peach.
This juicy, smooth-skinned fruit
Feels a prize within her reach.

**Florida's favorite fruit,
The ORANGE, to you and me,
Knows he's the King of Juice
And vitamins A and C !**

The PAPAYA has touched down.
It's produced in warm, wet places.
It's delicious color and flavor
Bring smiles to the judges' faces.

This entry's a real PEACH,
A rosy fruit with fuzz.
She's the sweetest and the juiciest
Fruit there ever was!

Here come the assorted PEARS,
The masters of disguises.
They ripen in the fall,
In different shapes and sizes.

The prickly PINEAPPLE'S next,
In sunny Hawaii it is found.
It makes a refreshing drink,
Or a cake that is baked upside down!

The next contestant's a PLUM,
So good on a hot afternoon.
When left out in the sun,
It soon shrivels into a PRUNE.

How many know that RAISINS
Are really dried up grapes?
They're wrinkled, brown and chewy,
So tasty in cookies and cakes.

**The STRAWBERRIES have entered The Bowl,
Believing that they will win.
They are the Queen of Shortcakes,
And the best jam you've ever been in!**

Here comes the TANGERINE,
So juicy and easy to peel,
Ripe around Thanksgiving,
And welcome at every meal.

At last we see the WATERMELONS,
The largest of the fruit,
As important to a picnic,
As pants are to a suit!

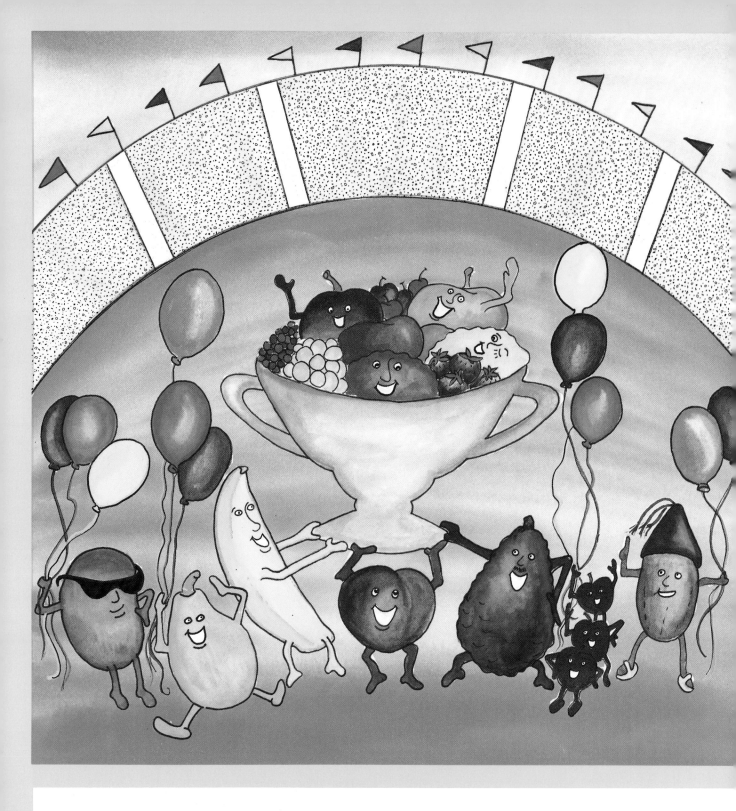

The judges can't agree . . .
For breakfast, lunch and dinner,
ALL the fruit are necessary
EVERYONE'S A WINNER !

Dianne Warren

earned her Bachelor of Arts Degree and Lifetime Elementary Teaching Credential from the University of California, Irvine. She has worked with students and teachers from preschool through junior college with an emphasis on Early Childhood Education. She has also been a consultant and sales representative for a major textbook company. Dianne lives with her husband in Florida where she conducts workshops on children and nutrition. She has also produced a nutrition-based coloring book, *Hop-A-Lot*, *The Healthy Habits Rabbit*. All books are available through oasis.dianne@juno.com

Susan Smith Jones

is a leading voice for healthy, balanced living in America today. She is the author of 12 books, including *Choose to Live Peacefully* and *A Fresh Start*, and over 500 magazine articles with her picture on several covers. For over 30 years, Susan taught health and fitness at UCLA. Her inspiring message and innovative techniques for achieving total health in body, mind and spirit have won her an enthusiastic following and have put her in high demand as a holistic health consultant and motivational speaker (lectures, workshops, keynote presentations) for community, corporate and church groups. A gifted teacher, Susan brings together modern research and ageless wisdom in all her work. (www.susansmithjones.com)

Amy Sorvaag Lindman

received a Bachelor of Commercial Art degree from the Oregon College of Art in Ashland, Oregon. Calligrapher and artist, Amy lives in central Washington with her husband and two daughters and her favorite fox terrier. Amy is a busy wife and mother, and makes times to be active in outdoor sports and physical fitness. Her creative work is inspired by living in the "Apple Capital of the World", which provides endless vistas of stunningly dramatic mountains and thousands of acres of orchards with their dozens of varieties of apples, pears, cherries, and other fruit.

If we gather all the vegetables,
And put them in a group,
Then simmer them with water
We'll make VEGETABLE SOUP!

Z is for ZUCCHINI,
A slender squash, so green,
Easily the most versatile
Vegetable ever seen.

Y is for those yummy **YAMS**,
And delicious **YELLOW SQUASH**, too.
Both keep muscles, bones and teeth
Working just like new!

X represents the caution we use
When choosing the foods that we eat.
Remembering never to eat in EXCESS,
Foods too fatty, salty or sweet.

W's for wonderful WATERCRESS
Growing wild along the stream.
Its wealth of important nutrients
Keep bones and teeth a winning team.

V is for VEGETABLES,
A few of nature's prizes.
They come in a variety of
Tastes, colors, shapes and sizes.

U is for UNDERGROUND,
Where potatoes grow,
With radishes and turnips
And carrots in a row.

T is for tasty TOMATOES,
A terrific source of vitamin A.
Eaten with veggies (but really a fruit),
They keep hair, skin and nails A-OK.

S is for savory SPINACH,
An important iron supplier,
Increasing our strength and energy,
So we run faster and jump higher!

R is for red **RADISHES**,
So flavorful and round.
This really rapid grower
You will find beneath the ground.

QUICKLY and QUIETLY
Are for the letter Q.
This is how your garden grows
Cucumbers for you.

P is for PEPPERS and PARSNIPS,
And pounds of POTATOES and PEAS.
With plenty of vegetables every day,
Our bodies perform with ease.

O is for outrageous ONIONS,
With their distinctive taste and smell.
Whether yellow, white, purple or green,
They clean our blood and help keep us well.

N is for NATURAL,
   The way nature intended:
   Nothing added or subtracted,
   Enriched or extended.

M is for marvelous MUSHROOMS,
That grow in moist, dark places.
We must carefully choose the ones that we eat,
To keep the smiles on our faces.

L is for leafy LETTUCE,
   Whose importance goes without question.
   Eating a salad every day,
   Ensures our food's proper digestion.

K is for a vegetable
From the cabbage family.
A king of iron and vitamins,
is KALE, to you and to me.

J is for jolly JACK-O-LANTERNS,
Carved from pumpkins so orange and so round
These jumbo members of the vegetable world
Keep our heart muscle healthy and sound.

I is for INCREDIBLE,
And how our health will be,
When eating veggies rich in iron,
For strength and energy.

H is for HEALTHY,
The way that we feel,
When served fruits or veggies
At every meal.

G is for glorious GARLIC,
Grown with its head in the ground.
It helps the body chase sickness away,
So we're healthy the total year-round.

F is for the FARMERS,
Who plant, water and hoe,
All the fabulous vegetables
That make our bodies grow.

E is for every EGGPLANT,
Helping our muscles, nerves and heart,
To do their jobs as best they can,
Keeping us happy, healthy and smart.

D is for the DELICIOUS
Vegetables we eat:
The corn and the celery,
The cabbage and the beet.

C is for clusters of CARROTS,
That help vision, especially at night.
Crunching on carrots every day
Is good jaw exercise bite after bite.

B is for bunches of BROCCOLI,
That build the body's defenses,
Keeping us healthy all of the time,
To run, play ball and climb fences.

A is for all the ASPARAGUS,
Alive with vitamin A.
For healthy hair, skin and eyes,
This vegetable leads the way.

To the children . . .
. . . and all their healthy tomorrows
Especially Margharita, Alicia,
Erica & Kimberly

This Book Belongs To

_____

Manufactured in the United States of America
Library of Congress Card Catalog Number: 99-69104
ISBN: 0-9652736-0-1
Illustrations: Amy Sorvaag Lindman
Cover design: Amy Sorvaag Lindman & Dianne Warren
Setup and typography: Robert Lefebvre

Publisher's Cataloging in Publication
(Prepared by Quality Books Inc.)

Warren, Dianne, 1947-
      Vegetable soup : the nutritional ABC's ; the fruit bowl : a
contest among the fruit / Dianne Warren and Susan Smith Jones ; Amy
Sorvaag Lindman, illustrator.
      p. cm.
      Titles from separate title page; works issued back-to-back and
inverted.
      SUMMARY: Pictures and verse about the benefits of fruits and
vegetables.
      Preassigned LCCN: 96-69740
      ISBN 0-9652736-0-1

      1. Vegetables–Juvenile poetry. 2. Fruit–Juvenile poetry. 3.
Alphabet rhymes. 4. Stories in rhyme. 5. Upside-down books. 6.
Toy and movable books. I. Jones, Susan Smith, 1950- II.
Lindman, Amy Sorvaag. III. Title. IV. Title: Fruit bowl.

PZ8.3.W3774Ve 1996   [E]
                                            QB196-40151

OASIS PUBLICATIONS

2344 Cambridge Dr
Sarasota, Florida 34232
Credit Card Orders 1-800-431-1579

VEGETABLE SOUP

The Nutritional ABC's

Dianne Warren
and
Susan Smith Jones

Illustrated by:
Amy Sorvaag Lindman

Food for Thought . . .

Our children look to us to show them how to live lives that are healthy and meaningful. Teaching them that natural foods are fun is an act of love and care. Teaching them that vegetables and fruits are their friends and allies is wonderful. *Vegetable Soup* and *The Fruit Bowl* serve this purpose beautifully.

John Robbins, *Author*
Diet for A New America and
Reclaiming Our Health

Children who grow up eating vegetables, fruit, grains and legumes, get a wonderful head start. People used to eat a lot of meat and dairy products — some people still do — but we now know that vegetarians are the healthiest people on the planet. As happy as the animals are that are not being eaten, our bodies are even happier with how healthy they feel.

Neal D. Barnard, M.D.
President Physicians Committee for
Responsible Medicine and *Author* of
Food For Life and *Eat Right, Live Longer*

Coronary heart disease begins in childhood. Also, children develop their taste preferences as they grow up. Therefore, parents would be wise to feed their children a vegetarian, or near vegetarian, diet. The authors of *Vegetable Soup* and *The Fruit Bowl* show us how.

Dean Ornish, M.D.
President and Director Preventive
Medicine Research Institute
Author, *Everyday Cooking with Dr. Dean Ornish*

We often forget that the cells of the brain consume more glucose, which is its source of energy, than any type of cell in the body. Additionally, many of the neurotransmitters that carry the messages from brain cell to brain cell are amino acids, the building blocks of proteins. It is not so far-fetched to acknowledge that nutrition is essential to growing children's brain biochemistry. A child's state of health is their state of nutrition. Educating our children to eat whole, unprocessed food with a minimum of additives and pesticides is probably the greatest lesson of all. Our children are so precious to us. Teaching them to eat for optimal health is a gift that will give back to us and others for a lifetime.

Donald J. Carrow, M.D.
Talk Radio's Medical Maverick
on *Here's to Your Health*

Food for Thought . . .

The need for books such as this could not be more urgent. We humans have a two-part brain: the primitive, or limbic brain, and the forebrain, or higher brain. The limbic brain is involved with the most basic needs of life: fight and flight reactions, territorial disputes, fear, defense, rage and the like. The higher brain is involved with intellectual functions, concepts of love, compassion, creativity and the higher pursuits of life. Nutritionally speaking, the limbic brain requires one-fifth the energy required by the higher brain. We are now into at least the second generation of kids raised on nutritionally bankrupt, junk foods. These diets only supply sufficient energy to feed the limbic brain, and not enough to feed the higher brain. And today we have the unprecedented phenomenon of kids bringing weapons to school creating terror in their homes and communities. We must feed our children a more nutritionally sound diet that nourishes the higher brain. Thank God there are books like *Vegetable Soup* and *The Fruit Bowl* to achieve that lofty goal.

Harvey Diamond, *Author*
Fit for Life and
You CAN Prevent Breast Cancer

Raising a child on a natural, vegetarian diet provides both good nutrition and valuable lessons in compassion, simplicity and personal responsibility. Children who learn to make smart choices about food grow into young adults with a better chance of making smart choices about life. *Vegetable Soup* and *The Fruit Bowl* are here to help.

Victoria Moran, *Author*
Get the Fat Out and
Shelter for the Spirit

Our bodies are made up of the food we eat. Fruit and vegetables are God's loving gifts to us. When we eat these foods we create healthy, loving bodies. *Vegetable Soup* and *The Fruit Bowl* help us, as parents and teachers, to build this awareness in our children. The choice is ours. We can improve our health by choosing to eat these precious gifts.

Dr. Wayne W. Dyer, *Lecturer/Author*
Your Erroneous Zones and
Your Sacred Self

Food manufacturers are spending billions of dollars to encourage children (and adults) to become dependent upon processed and restaurant foods, which are all too unhealthy. In fact, many children will never learn how to cook. It is vitally important for adults to teach kids about food, about nutrition, and how to cook. That will open up a whole new (and delicious) world that kids will enjoy for the rest of their lives.

Michael Jacobson, PhD
Executive Director
Center for Science in the Public Interest